BOB MARLEY
FOR UKULELE

ISBN 978-1-4803-9523-7

HAL•LEONARD®
CORPORATION

7777 W. BLUEMOUND RD. P.O. BOX 13819 MILWAUKEE, WI 53213

Visit Hal Leonard Online at
www.halleonard.com

CONTENTS

Buffalo Soldier

Words and Music by Noel Williams and Bob Marley

First note

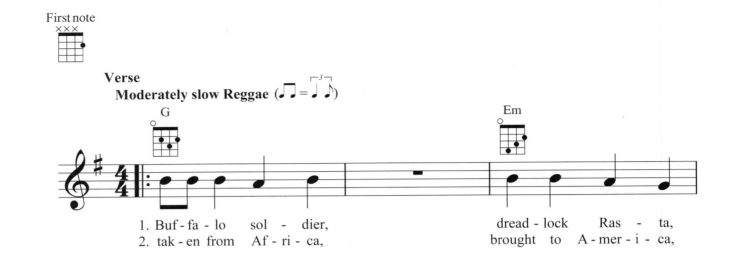

Verse
Moderately slow Reggae

1. Buf - fa - lo sol - dier,   dread - lock Ras - ta,
2. tak - en from Af - ri - ca,   brought to A - mer - i - ca,

there was a buf - fa - lo sol - dier   in the
fight - ing on ar - riv - al,

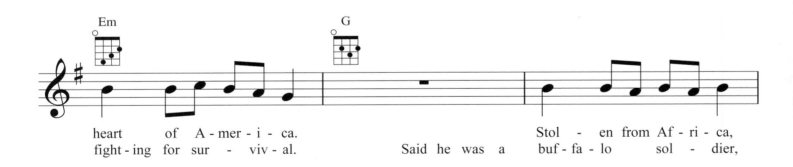

heart of A - mer - i - ca.   Stol - en from Af - ri - ca,
fight - ing for sur - viv - al.   Said he was a buf - fa - lo sol - dier,

brought to A - mer - i - ca;
dread - lock Ras - ta,

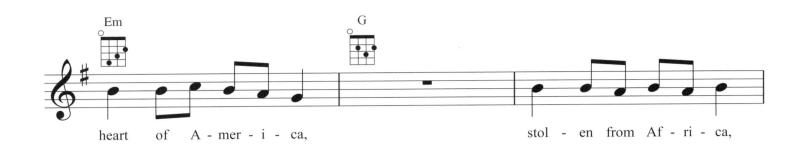

heart of A - mer - i - ca, stol - en from Af - ri - ca,

brought to A - mer - i - ca. Said he was

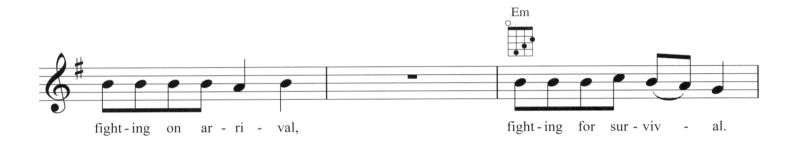

fight - ing on ar - ri - val, fight - ing for sur - viv - al.

Said he was the buf - fa - lo sol - dier, win the

Chorus

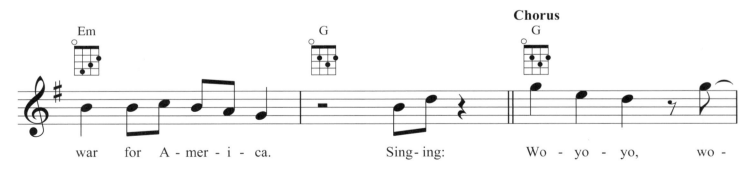

war for A - mer - i - ca. Sing - ing: Wo - yo - yo, wo -

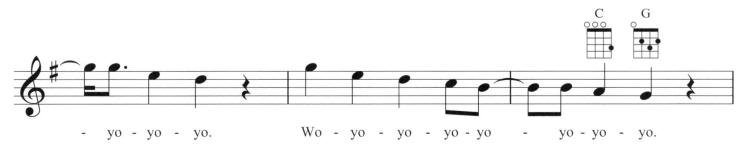

- yo - yo - yo. Wo - yo - yo - yo - yo - yo - yo - yo.

Exodus

Words and Music by Bob Marley

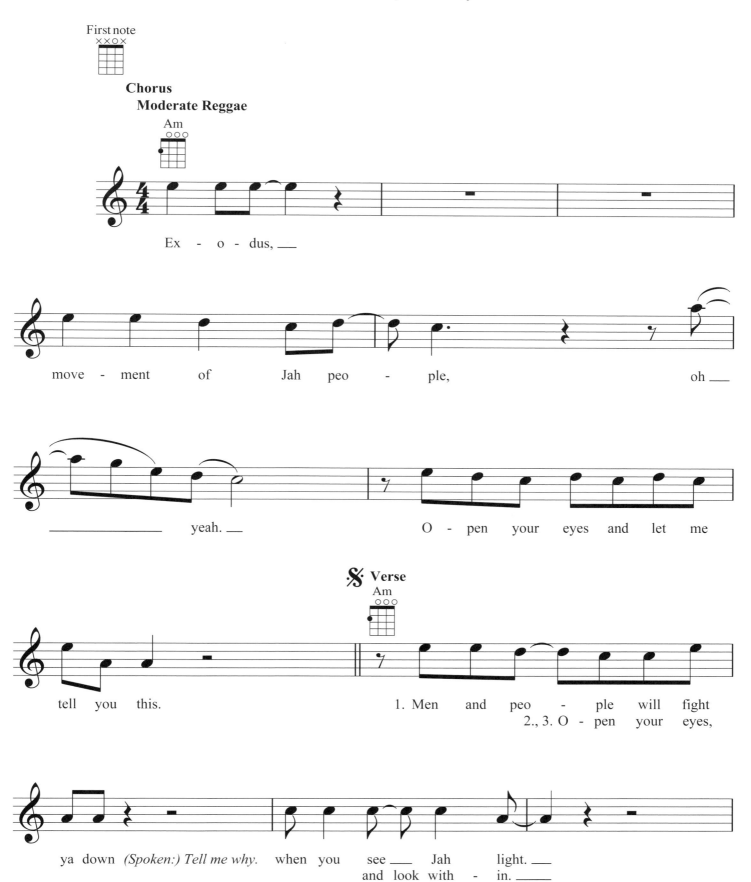

Let me tell you, if you're not wrong, *(Spoken:) Then why?*
Are you sat - is - fied

ev - 'ry - thing is al - right.
with the life you're liv - ing?

So we gon - na

walk,
We know where __ we're go - ing.

al - right, __

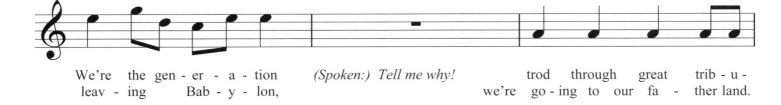

through the roads __ of cre - a - tion.
We know where __ we're __ from. __

We're

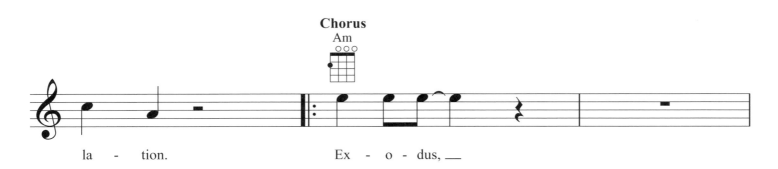

We're the gen - er - a - tion
leav - ing Bab - y - lon,

(Spoken:) Tell me why!

trod through great trib - u -
we're go - ing to our fa - ther land.

Chorus

Am

la - tion.

Ex - o - dus, __

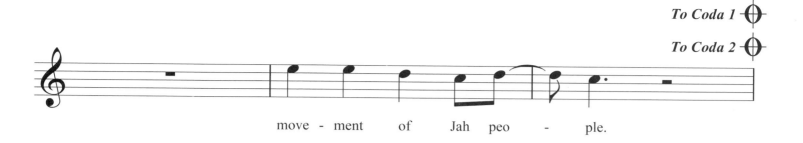

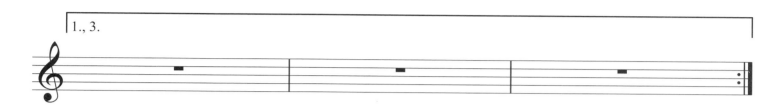

move - ment of Jah peo - ple.

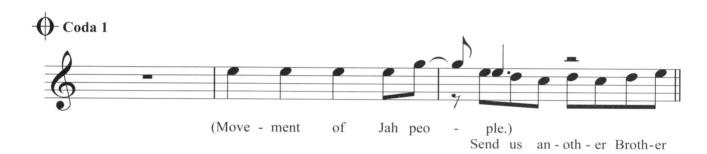

Coda 1

(Move - ment of Jah peo - ple.)

Send us an - oth - er Broth-er

Bridge

Am

(Move - ment of Jah peo - ple.)

Mo - ses. Gon - na cross __ the Red __ Sea. __

1.

(Move - ment of Jah peo - ple.)

Send us an - oth - er Broth - er

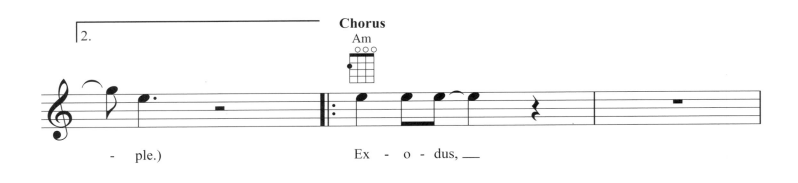

Chorus

- ple.)   Ex - o - dus, —

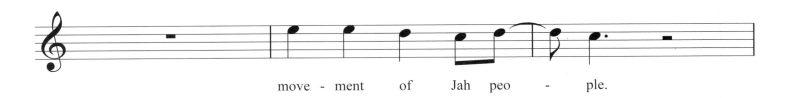

move - ment of Jah peo - ple.

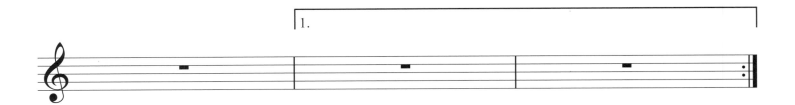

1.

2.

**D.S. al Coda 2
(with repeat)**

Interlude

Coda 2

Move - ment of Jah peo -

- ple;   move - ment of Jah peo - ple.

Bridge

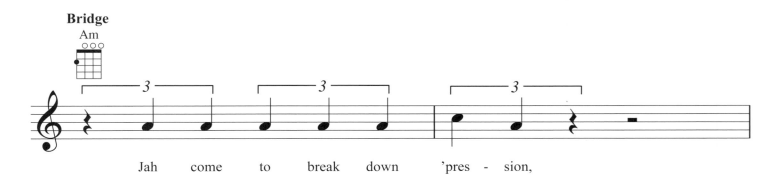

3   3   3

Jah come to break down 'pres - sion,

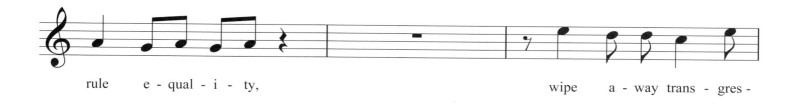

rule   e - qual - i - ty,   wipe   a - way trans - gres -

sion,   set   the   cap - tives   free. _____

Chorus

Am

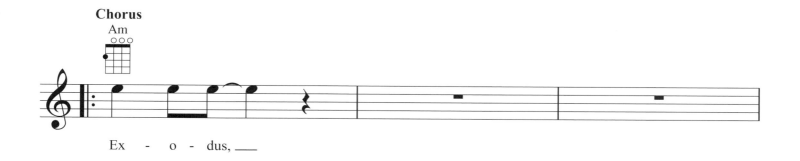

Ex - o - dus, ___

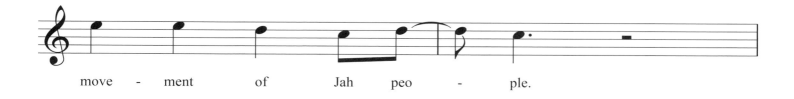

move - ment   of   Jah   peo - ple.

Outro

Am

Repeat and fade

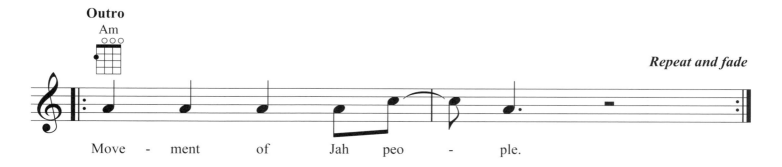

Move - ment   of   Jah   peo - ple.

Could You Be Loved

Words and Music by Bob Marley

First note

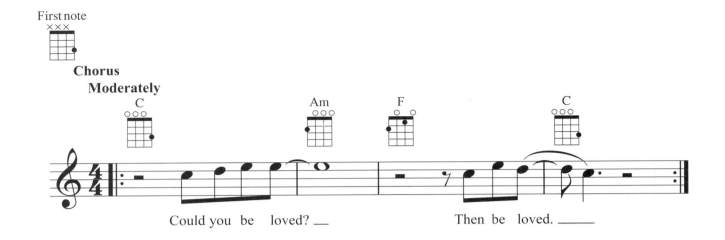

Chorus
Moderately

Could you be loved? ___ Then be loved. _____

1. Don't let ___ them fool ___ ya,
2. Don't let ___ them change _ ya,

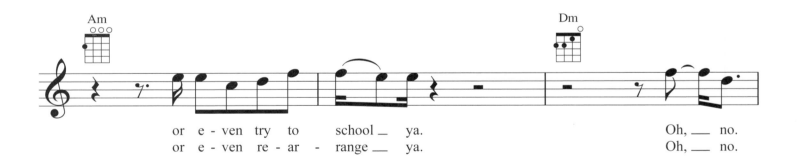

or e - ven try to school _ ya.   Oh, ___ no.
or e - ven re - ar - range ___ ya.   Oh, ___ no.

We've got a mind of our own. ___ So, go
We've got a life to live. ___

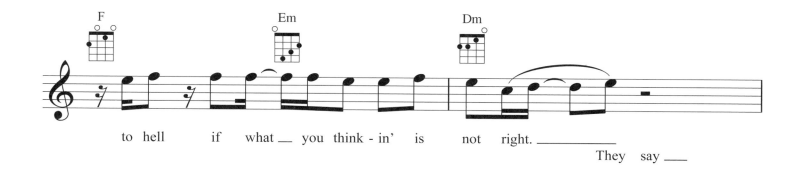

to hell   if   what __ you think - in'   is   not   right. _____
                                                                    They   say __

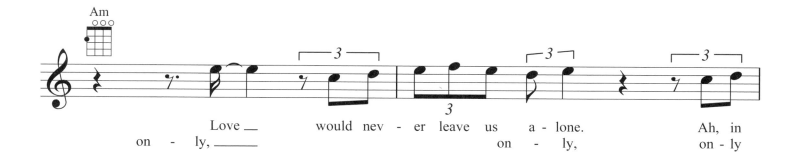

Love __   would nev - er   leave   us   a - lone.   Ah, in
on - ly, _____   on - ly,   on - ly

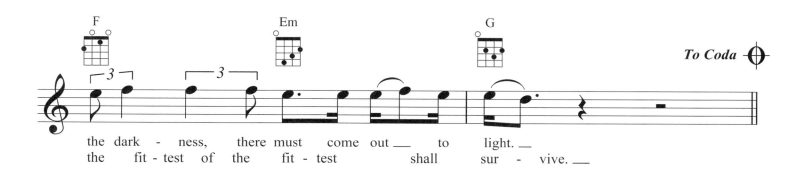

To Coda ⊕

the   dark - ness,   there   must   come   out __   to   light. __
the   fit - test   of   the   fit - test   shall   sur - vive. __

Chorus

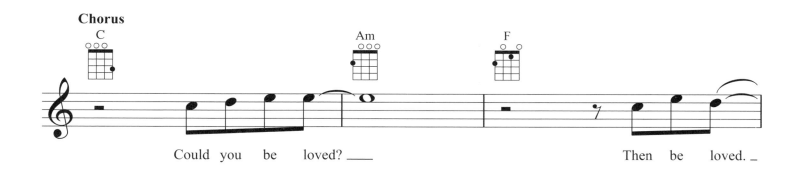

Could   you   be   loved? ____   Then   be   loved. __

_____   Now, could   you   be   loved? ____   Whoa, __

____ yeah,   then be loved. _____

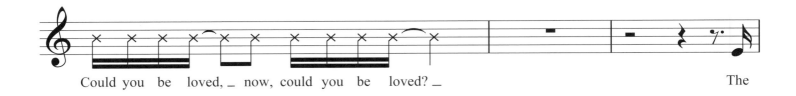

Could you be loved, _ now, could you be loved? _   The

road of life is rock - y   and   you may stum - ble, too. ___   So,

why don't you point your fin - gers at some - one   else that's judg - ing you?   Love _

____ your broth - er,   man. _
(Could you be,   could you be,   could you be loved?   Could you be, could you be loved?

Could you be, could you be, could you be loved? Could you be, could you be loved?)

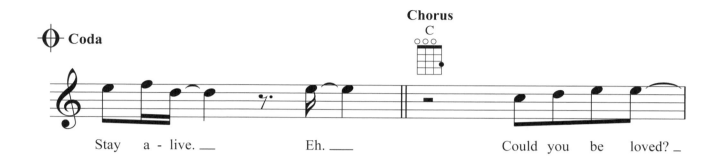

Stay a - live. ___ Eh. ___ Could you be loved? _

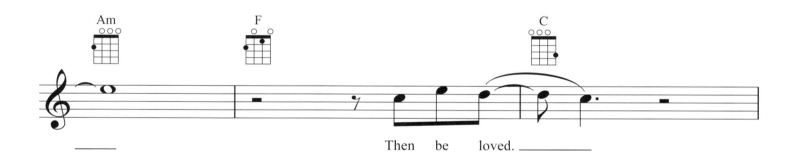

___ Then be loved. _____

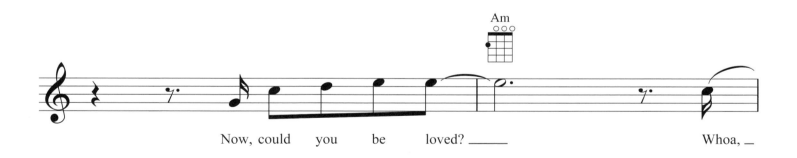

Now, could you be loved? _____ Whoa, _

___ yeah, then be loved. _____

Get Up Stand Up

Words and Music by Bob Marley and Peter Tosh

I know you don't know what ___ life is real-ly worth. He said all ___
take a-way ev-'ry-thing and make ___ ev-'ry-bod-y feel high.

___ that glit-ter is gold. ___ Half ___ that sto-ry ain't nev-er been told. ___ So
But if you know what life is worth, you will look for yours on earth. And

2nd time, D.C. al Coda

now you see ___ the light, ___ eh. You stand up for ___ your right. Come on!
now you see ___ the light. ___ You stand up for ___ your right. Jah!

Coda

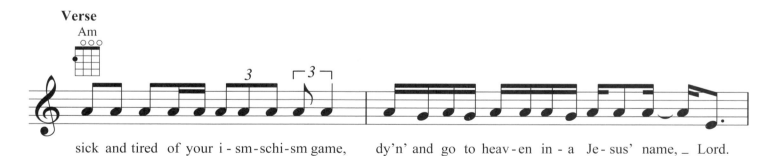

Don't give up ___ the fight. 3. We're

Verse

Am

sick and tired of your i - sm-schi-sm game, dy'n' and go to heav-en in - a Je-sus' name, ___ Lord.

We know ___ and we un-der-stand. ___ Al-might-y God is a liv-ing Man. ___ You can

fool some peo - ple some - times, but you can't fool all ___ the peo - ple all the time. ___ So

now we see ___ the light. We gon - na stand up for ___ our rights. So ___ you bet - ter

Outro-Chorus

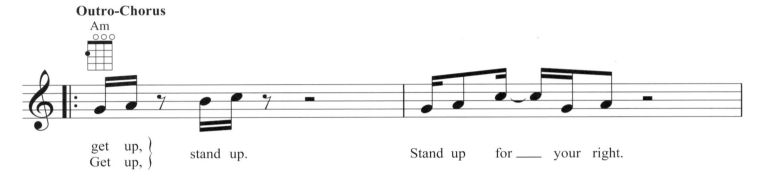

get up,
Get up, } stand up.   Stand up for ___ your right.

Get up, stand up.   Don't give up ___ the fight.

Get up, stand up.   Stand up for ___ your right.

Repeat and fade

Get up, stand up.   Don't give up ___ the fight.

Lively Up Yourself

Words and Music by Bob Marley

Chorus

I Know a Place

(Where We Can Carry On)

Words and Music by Bob Marley and Rita Marley

First note

1. When the whole world lets you down __

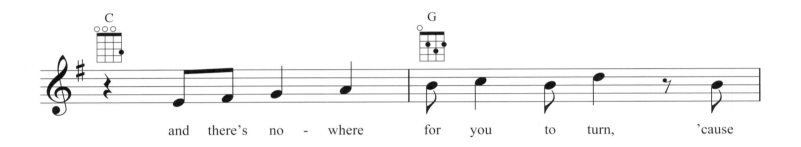

and there's no - where for you to turn, 'cause

all of your best friends let you down. __

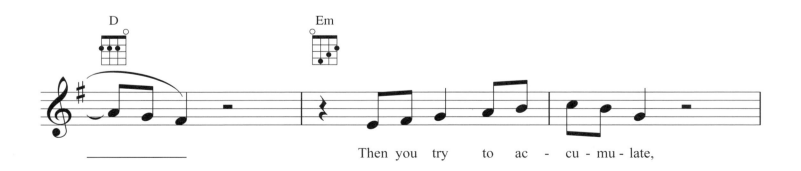

Then you try to ac - cu - mu - late,

but the world is full of hate, ___ so all of your best thoughts

just a - drift through ___ space. _____

Chorus

I know a place ___ where we can car - ry on. ___

___ I know a place ___ where

we can car - ry on. ___ We can car - ry on, ___

we can car - ry on. _____

I Shot the Sheriff

Words and Music by Bob Marley

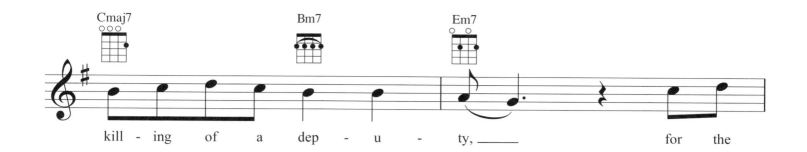

kill - ing of a dep - u - ty, _____ for the

Interlude

life of a dep - u - ty. __ But I say: __ *(Instrumental)*

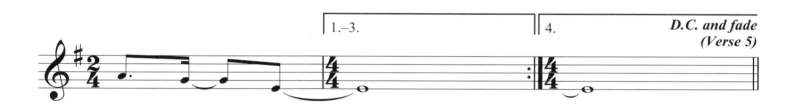

Additional Lyrics

2. I shot the sheriff, but I swear it was in self-defense.
   I shot the sheriff, and they say it is a capital offense.
   Sheriff John Brown always hated me; for what, I don't know.
   Every time that I plant a seed, he said, "Kill it before it grows."
   He said, "Kill it before it grows." But I say:

3. I shot the sheriff, but I swear it was in self-defense.
   I shot the sheriff, but I swear it was in self-defense.
   Freedom came my way one day, and I started out of town.
   All of a sudden, I see Sheriff John Brown aiming to shoot me down.
   So I shot, I shot him down. But I say:

4. I shot the sheriff, but I did not shoot the deputy.
   I shot the sheriff, but I did not shoot the deputy.
   Reflexes got the better of me, and what is to be must be.
   Every day, the bucket goes to the well, but one day the bottom will drop out.
   Yes, one day the bottom will drop out. But I say:

5. I shot the sheriff, but I didn't shoot the deputy.
   I shot the sheriff, but I did not shoot no deputy.
   Instrumental fade

Iron Lion Zion

Words and Music by Bob Marley

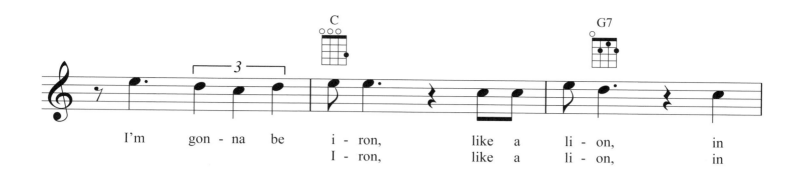

I'm gon-na be i - ron, like a li - on, in
I - ron, like a li - on, in

To Coda

Zi - on, oh yeah. ___
Zi - on."

1.

2.

Li - on, i - ron, Zi - on, li - on, Zi - on.
I - ron, li - on, Zi - on.

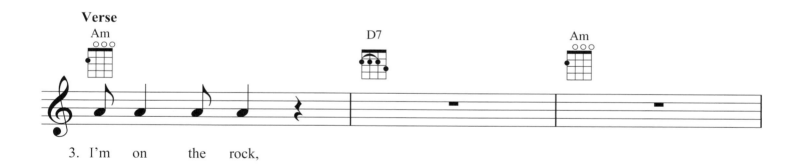

Verse

3. I'm on the rock,

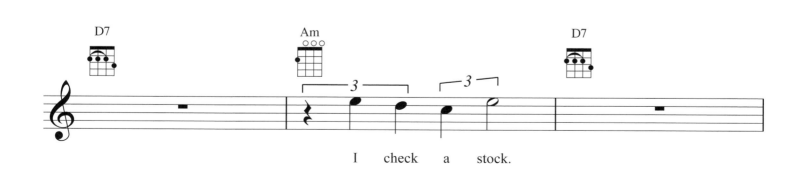

I check a stock.

I had to run like a fu - gi - tive ___

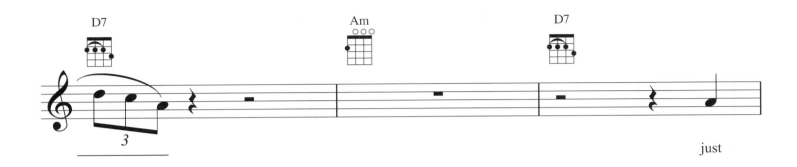

just

to, just to save the life ___ I live, _____ oh, now.

Chorus

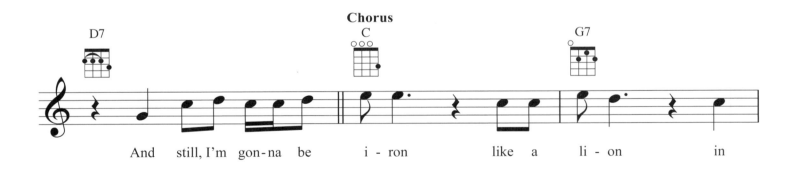

And still, I'm gon-na be i - ron like a li - on in

Zi - on. I'm gon - na be i - ron like a

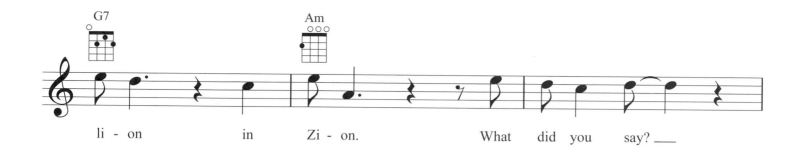

li - on   in   Zi - on.   What did you   say? ___

D.S. al Coda

I - ron,   li - on,   Zi - on.

Coda

Steal them off of me.   I - ron, li - on, Zi - on.

I - ron, li - on, Zi - on.   I'm on the run.

Got no gun.   I - ron, li - on, Zi - on.

Is This Love

Words and Music by Bob Marley

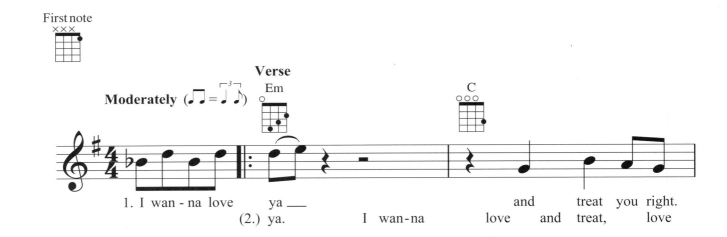

1. I wan-na love ya ___ and treat you right.
(2.) ya. I wan-na love and treat, love

I wan-na love ya ___ I wan-na love ya ___ ev-er-y
and treat you right. ___ ev-'ry ___

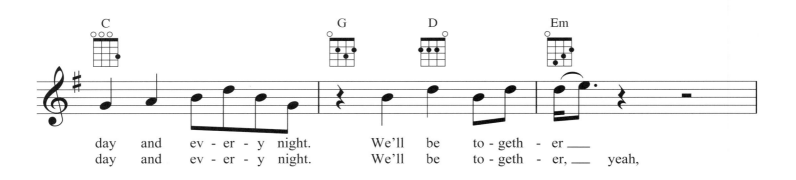

day and ev-er-y night. We'll be to-geth-er ___
day and ev-er-y night. We'll be to-geth-er, ___ yeah,

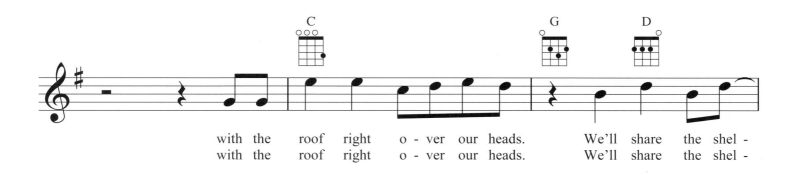

with the roof right o-ver our heads. We'll share the shel-
with the roof right o-ver our heads. We'll share the shel-

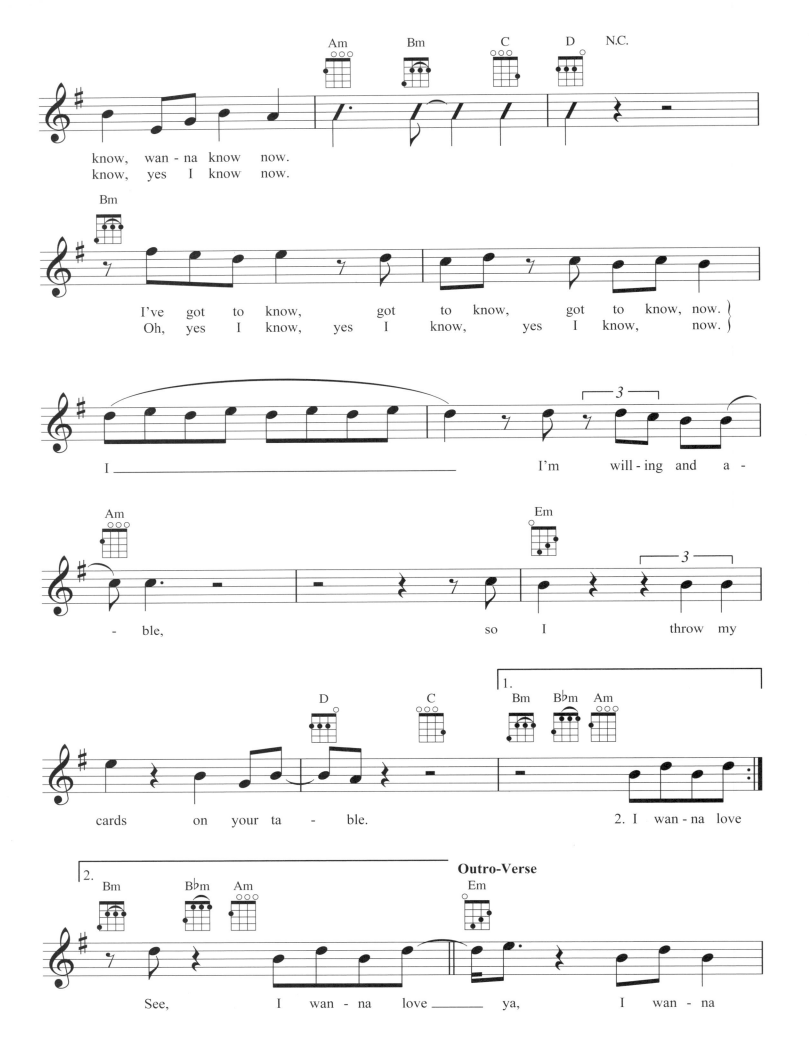

love and treat ya, love and treat you right. I wan-na love

ya ev-er-y day and ev-er-y night. We'll be to-geth-

-er with the roof right o-ver our heads.

We'll share the shel - ter

of my sin-gle bed. We'll share the same ___ room, yeah. ___

Repeat and fade

Jah pro-vides the bread. We'll share the shel-

39

Jamming

Words and Music by Bob Marley

First note

Chorus
Moderate Reggae feel

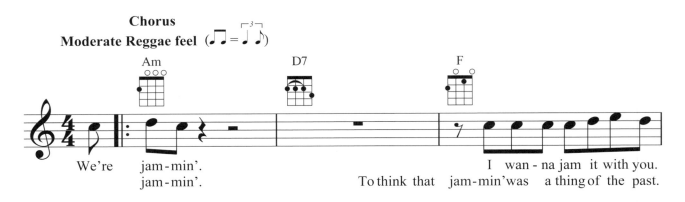

We're   jam-min'.
            jam-min'.
                                        I   wan-na jam it with you.
                        To think that jam-min'was a thing of the past.

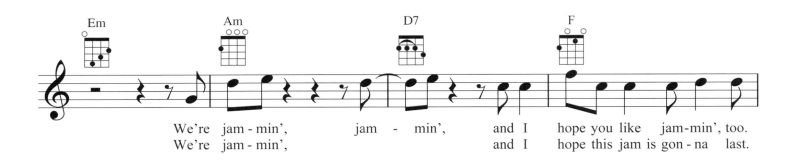

We're jam-min',   jam-min',   and I   hope you like jam-min', too.
We're jam-min',   and I   hope this jam is gon-na last.

Verse

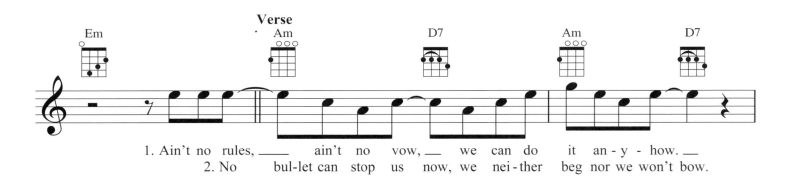

1. Ain't no rules, ____ ain't no vow, __ we can do   it an-y-how. __
2. No   bul-let can stop us now, we nei-ther beg nor we won't bow.

I and I will see you through. _   'Cause ev-er-y day we pay the price, we're the
Nei-ther can be bought nor sold. ____   We all de-fend the right, Jah, Jah,

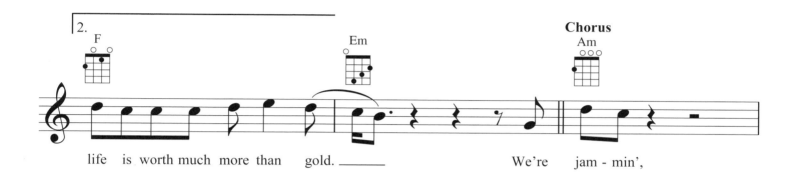

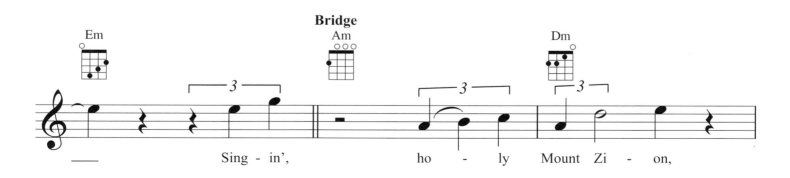

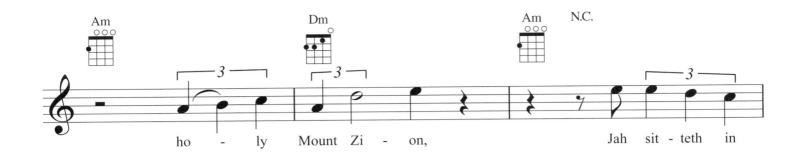

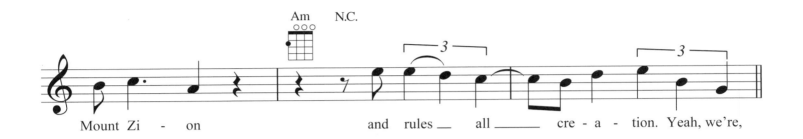

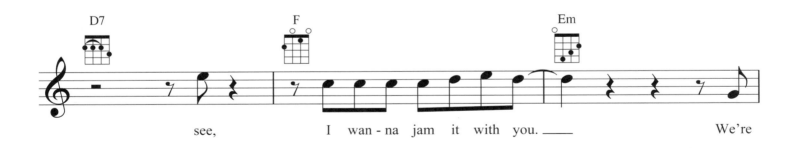

Verse

3. Jah knows how much I've tried, the truth I can-not hide

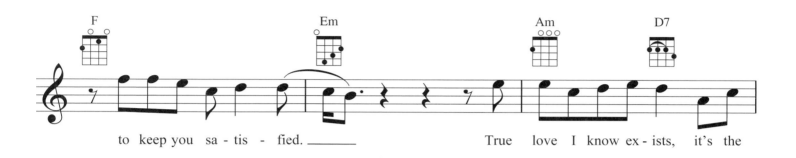

to keep you sa - tis - fied. _____ True love I know ex - ists, it's the

love I can't re - sist, so jam by my side. _____ We're

Outro-Chorus

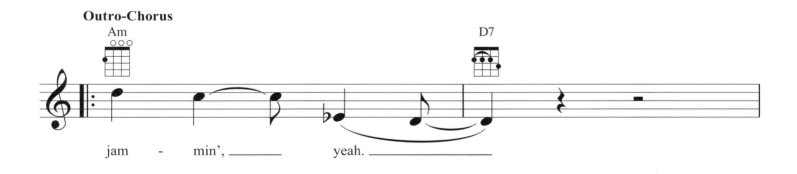

jam - min', _____ yeah. _____

Repeat ad lib. and fade

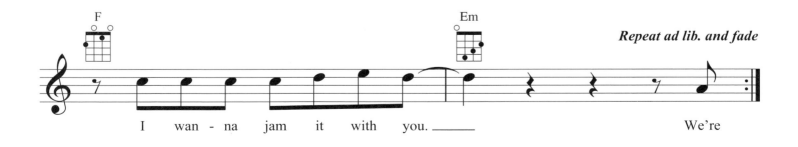

I wan - na jam it with you. _____ We're

No Woman No Cry

Words and Music by Vincent Ford

hyp - o - crites   as they would   min - gle with the good peo - ple we

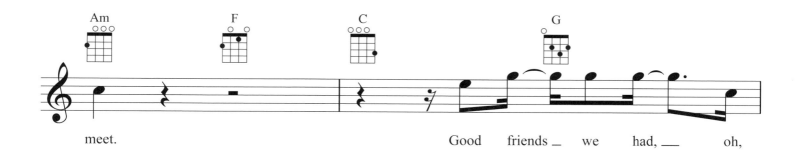

meet.   Good friends __ we had, __ oh,

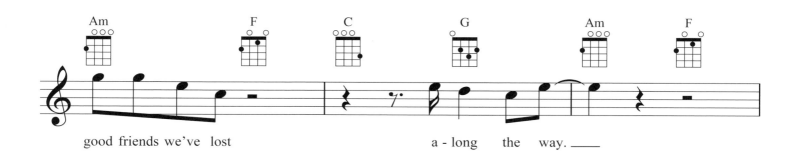

good friends we've lost   a - long the way. ____

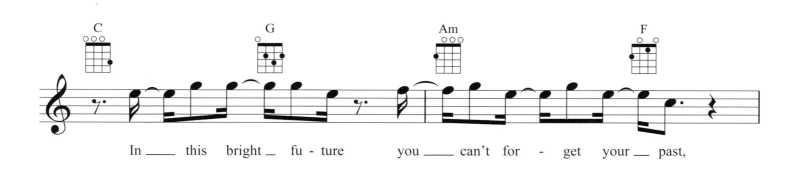

In ____ this bright __ fu - ture   you ____ can't for - get your __ past,

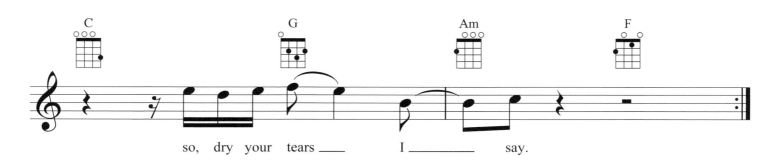

so, dry your tears ____ I _____ say.

Additional Lyrics

2. Said, I remember when we used to sit
   In the government yard in Trenchtown.
   And then Georgie would make a firelight
   As it was log wood burnin' through the night.
   Then we would cook cornmeal porridge,
   Of which I'll share with you.
   My feet is my only carriage,
   So, I've got to push on through.
   But while I'm gone, I mean...

Redemption Song

Words and Music by Bob Marley

Additional Lyrics

2., 3. Emancipate yourselves from mental slavery;
None but ourselves can free our minds.
Have no fear for atomic energy,
'Cause none of them can stop the time.
How long shall they kill our prophets
While we stand aside and look?
Some say it's just a part of it;
We've got to fulfill the Book.

One Love

Words and Music by Bob Marley

Roots, Rock, Reggae

Words and Music by Vincent Ford

this a reg - gae mu - sic.

Roots, Rock, __ Reg - gae, _____ yeah, __ this a reg - gae mu - sic.

Play I some mu - sic, _____

this a reg - gae mu - sic. Play I some

mu - sic, this a reg - gae mu - sic.

Bridge

Play I on the R and B, _____ want all my peo - ple to see.

Satisfy My Soul

Words and Music by Bob Marley

First note

Verse
Reggae

1. Oh, please   don't you rock   my boat __

'cause I don't   want my boat   to

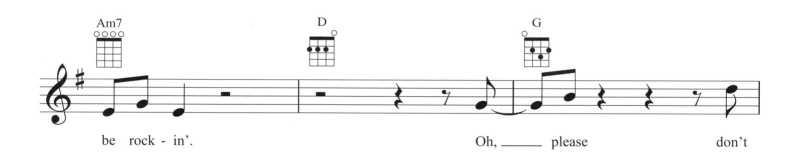

be rock - in'.   Oh, ___ please   don't

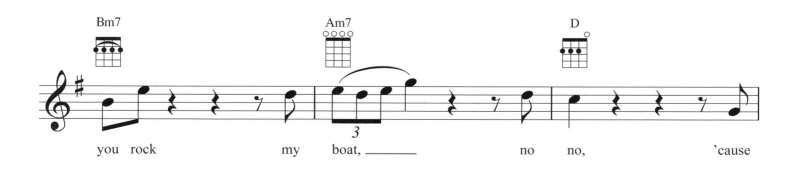

you rock   my boat, ___ no no,   'cause

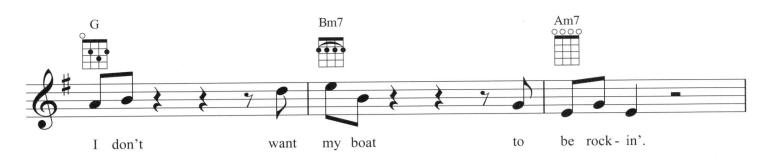

I don't want my boat to be rock-in'.

Pre-Chorus

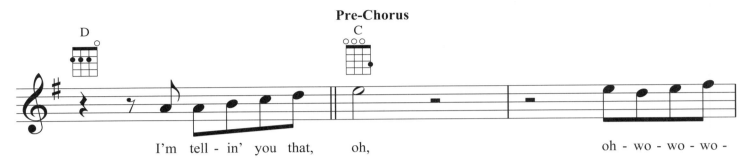

I'm tell-in' you that, oh, oh - wo - wo - wo -

wo, I like it, like it like this. So

keep it stiff ___ like _____ this. And you should

know, you should know by now I

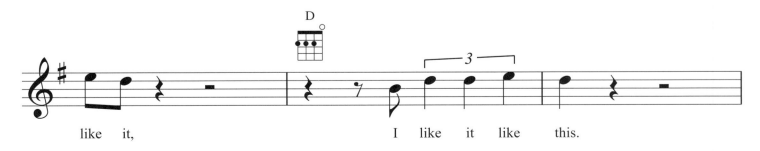

like it, I like it like this.

feel like a sweep-stake win-ner.
hold me tight, you make me feel al-right.

Can't you see?

(1.) You must be-lieve me.
(2.–4.) Why won't you be-lieve me?

Oh, dar-

To Coda ⊕ | 1., 3.

- ling, dar-ling, I'm call-ing, call-ing.

2.
D.S. al Coda
(with repeat)

- ing, call-ing.

⊕ *Coda*

- ing, call-ing.

Outro
Am7

Sat-is-fy —

D

Repeat and fade

—— my soul.

Sat-is-fy —— my soul.

So Much Trouble in the World

Words and Music by Bob Marley

First note
XXOX

Chorus
Moderate Reggae

So much _ trou - ble in the world. _____

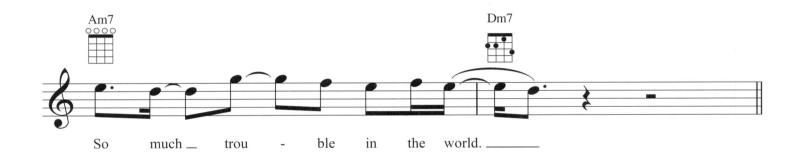

So much _ trou - ble in the world. _____

Verse

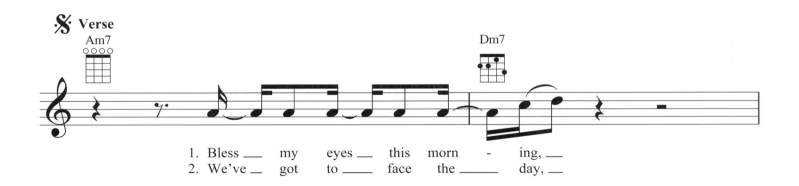

1. Bless _ my eyes _ this morn - ing, _
2. We've _ got to _ face the _____ day, _

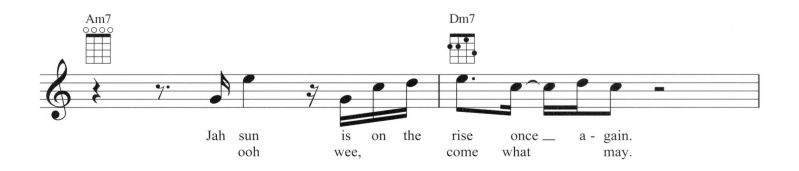

Jah sun   is on the   rise once _ a - gain.
ooh   wee,   come what _ may.

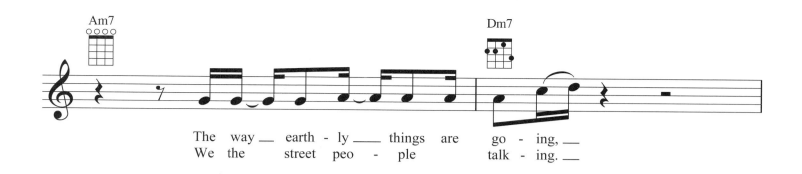

The way — earth - ly — things are go - ing, —
We the street peo - ple talk - ing. —

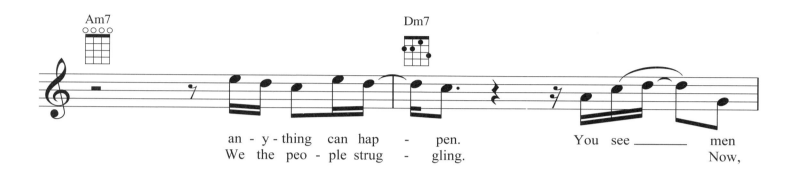

an - y - thing can hap - pen. You see _____ men
We the peo - ple strug - gling. Now,

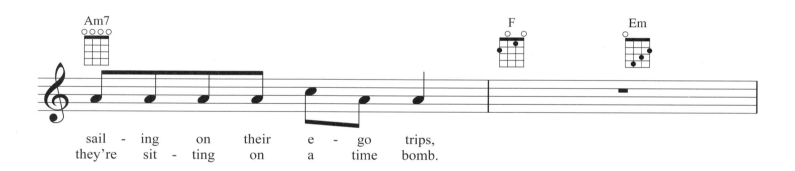

sail - ing on their e - go trips,
they're sit - ting on a time bomb.

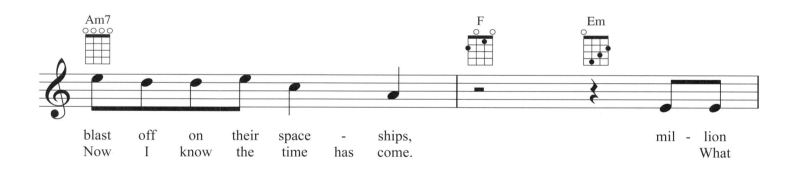

blast off on their space - ships, mil - lion
Now I know the time has come. What

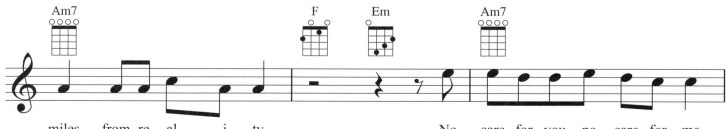

miles from re - al - i - ty. No care for you, no care for me.
goes on up is com - ing on down. Goes a - round and comes a - round.

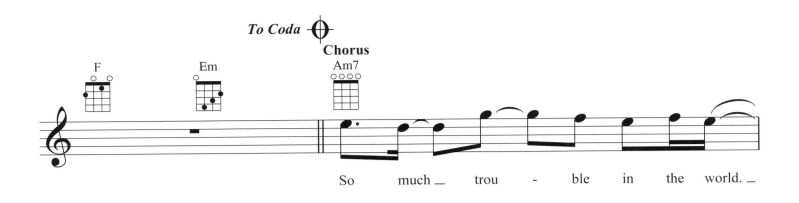

So much __ trou - ble in the world. __

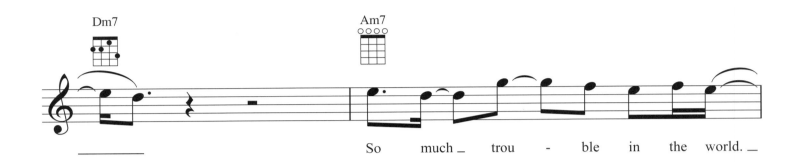

__ So much __ trou - ble in the world. __

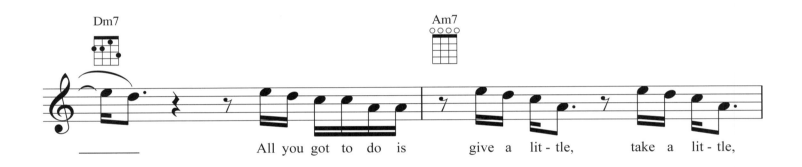

__ All you got to do is give a lit - tle, take a lit - tle,

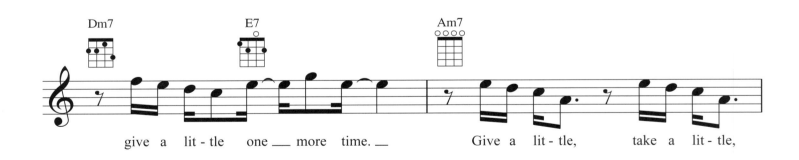

give a lit - tle one __ more time. __ Give a lit - tle, take a lit - tle,

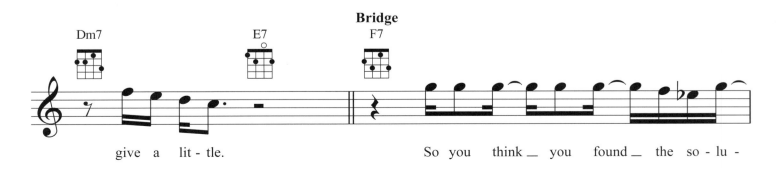

give a lit - tle. So you think __ you found __ the so - lu -

- tion.   But it's __ just an - oth - er il - lu -

- sion.   So be - fore __ you check out this tide,

G7

D.S. al Coda

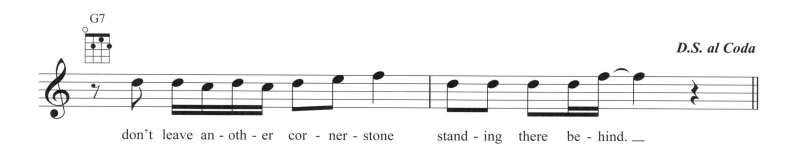

don't leave an - oth - er cor - ner - stone   stand - ing there be - hind. __

Coda
Outro-Chorus

Am7   Dm7

{ So }
{ so }   much __ trou - ble in the world. _____

Am7   Dm7

Repeat and fade

So   much __ trou - ble in the world. _____   There is

Stir It Up

Words and Music by Bob Marley

First note

Intro
Moderate Reggae

Play 4 times   **Chorus**

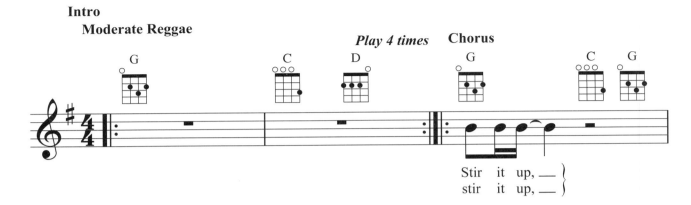

Stir it up, —
stir it up, —

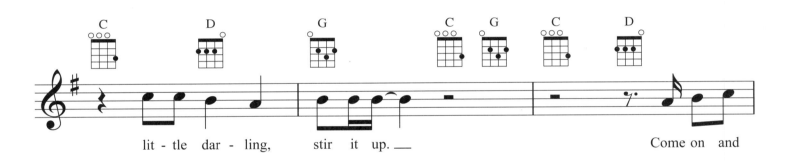

lit - tle dar - ling,   stir it up. —   Come on and

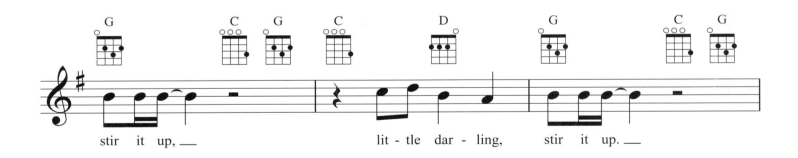

stir it up, —   lit - tle dar - ling,   stir it up. —

Verse

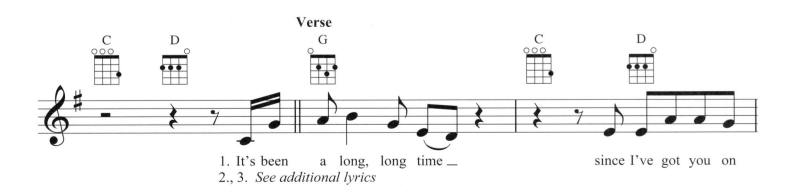

1. It's been   a long, long time —   since I've got you on
2., 3. *See additional lyrics*

Sun Is Shining

Words and Music by Bob Marley

(Wed'n-s'day morn - ing,) tell my-self a new day is ris-ing.

(Thurs - day eve - ning;) get on the rise, a new day is dawn-ing.

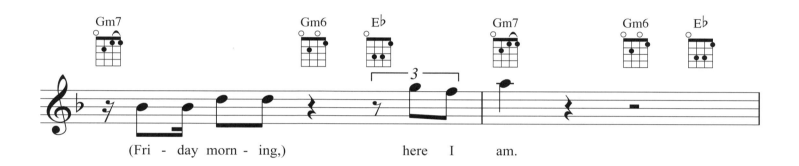

(Fri - day morn - ing,) here I am.

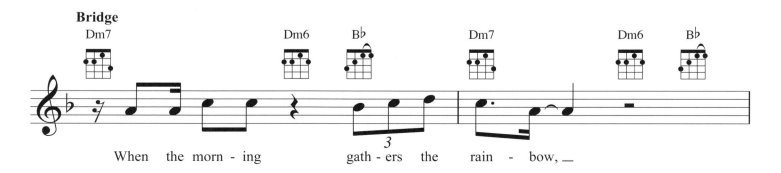

(Sat-ur-day eve - ning,) want you to know just, ___ want you ___ to know just where I stand. _

Bridge

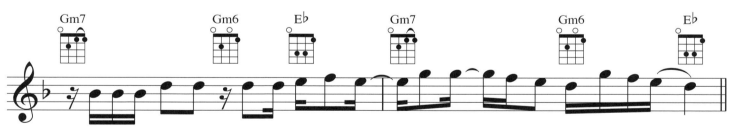

When the morn - ing gath - ers the rain - bow, _

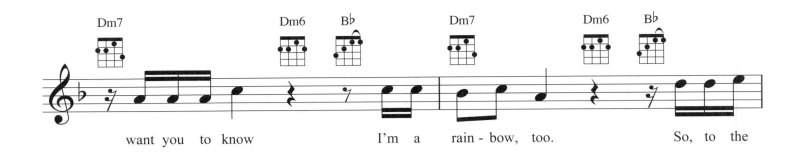

want you to know   I'm a   rain - bow, too.   So, to the

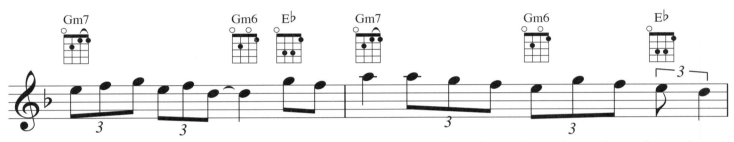

res - cue,   here I am.   Want you

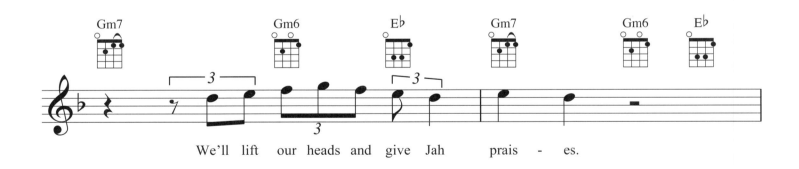

to know just, if you can, __ where I   stand, know, know, know, know, know, know, know, know.

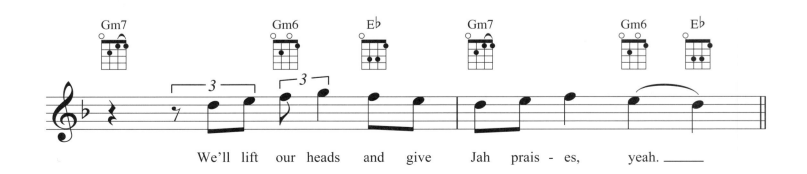

We'll lift   our heads and give Jah   prais - es.

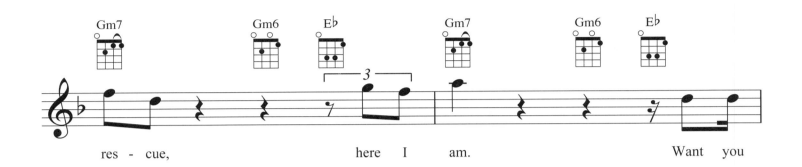

We'll lift   our heads   and   give   Jah prais - es,   yeah. _____

Chorus

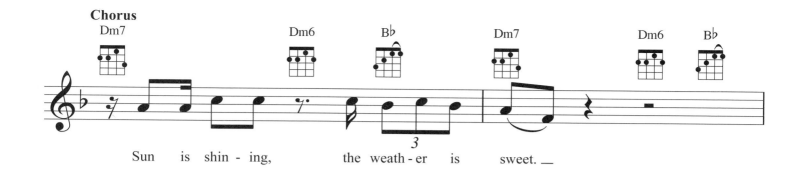

Sun is shin - ing, the weath - er is sweet. __

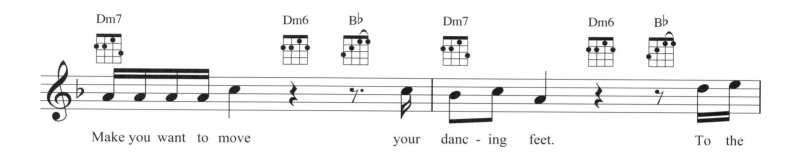

Make you want to move your danc - ing feet. To the

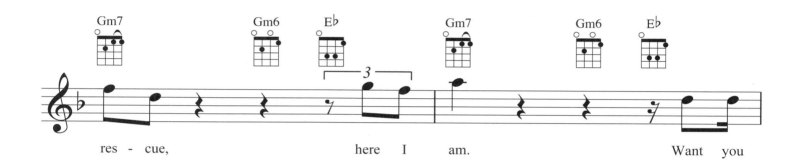

res - cue, here I am. Want you

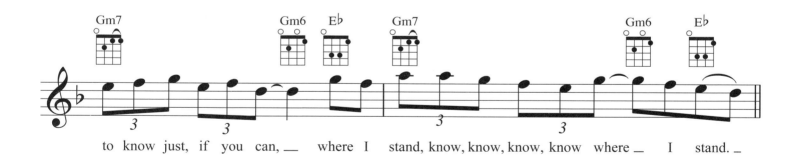

to know just, if you can, __ where I stand, know, know, know, know where __ I stand. __

Outro   *Repeat and fade*

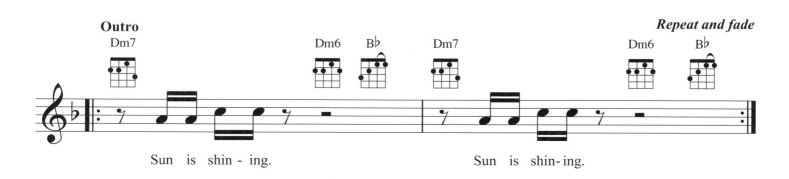

Sun is shin - ing.   Sun is shin - ing.

Waiting in Vain

Words and Music by Bob Marley

First note

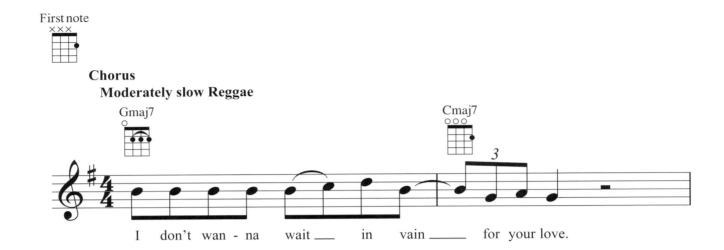

Chorus
Moderately slow Reggae

I don't wan - na wait ___ in vain ___ for your love.

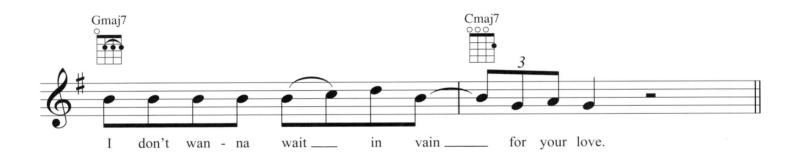

I don't wan - na wait ___ in vain ___ for your love.

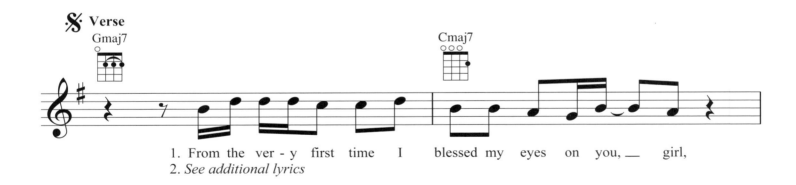

Verse

1. From the ver - y first time I blessed my eyes on you, ___ girl,
2. *See additional lyrics*

my ___ heart says, ___ "Fol - low ___ through."

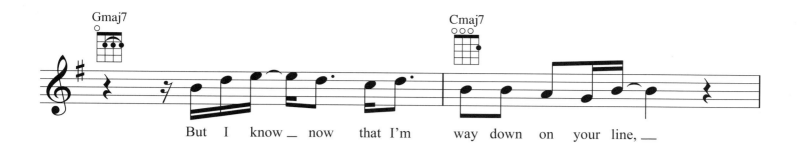

But I know __ now that I'm way down on your line, __

but the wait - ing feel is fine. ____

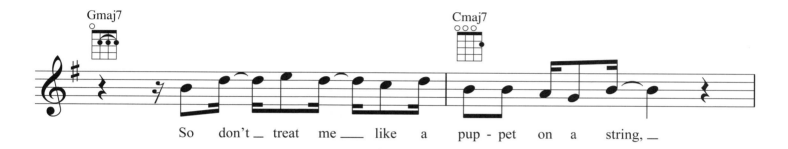

So don't __ treat me ____ like a pup - pet on a string, __

'cause I know how to do my thing.

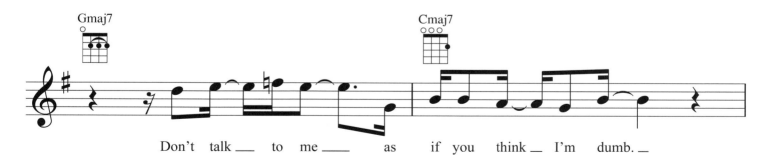

Don't talk __ to me ____ as if you think __ I'm dumb. __

I wan - na know when you're gon - na come. ____ See,

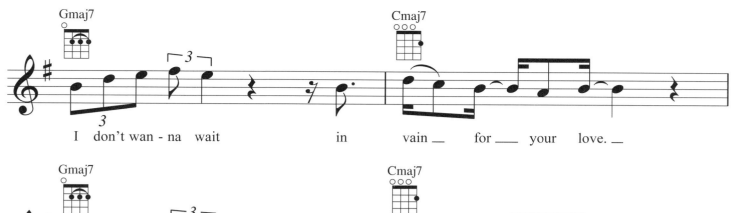

I don't wan-na wait   in   vain __ for __ your love. __

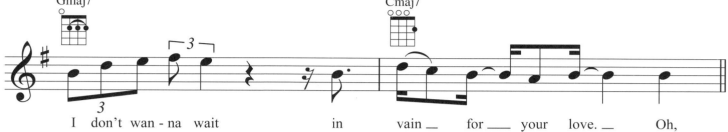

I don't wan-na wait   in   vain __ for __ your love. __   Oh,

Outro

I don't wan-na, I don't wan-na, I don't wan-na, I don't wan-na, I don't wan-na wait in vain. _   No,

I don't wan-na, I don't wan-na, I don't wan-na, I don't wan-na, I don't wan-na wait in vain. _   It's your

Repeat and fade

love that I'm __ wait-ing on.   It's my   love that you're run-ning from. _   It's your

Additional Lyrics

2. It's been three years since I'm knockin' on your door,
And I still can knock some more.
Ooh girl, ooh girl, is it feasible,
I wanna know now, for I to knock some more?
Ya see, in life I know there is lots of grief,
But your love is my relief.
Tears in my eyes burn,
Tears in my eyes burn while I'm waiting,
While I'm waiting for my turn.

Three Little Birds

Words and Music by Bob Marley

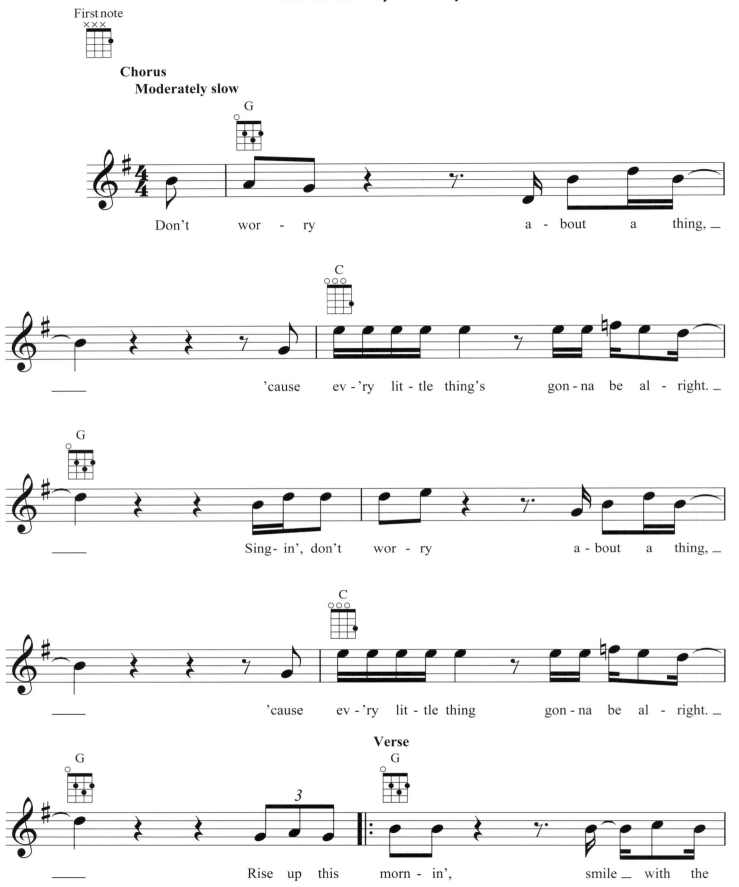

ris - ing sun. Three __ lit - tle birds, ___ pitched by my

door - step. Sing - in' sweet __ songs, of mel - o - dies

pure and true, say - in', "This is my mes - sage to you." __

Chorus

___ Sing - in', don't wor - ry a - bout a thing, __

___ 'cause ev - 'ry lit - tle thing is gon - na be al - right. __

___ Sing - in', don't wor - ry, don't wor - ry 'bout a thing, __

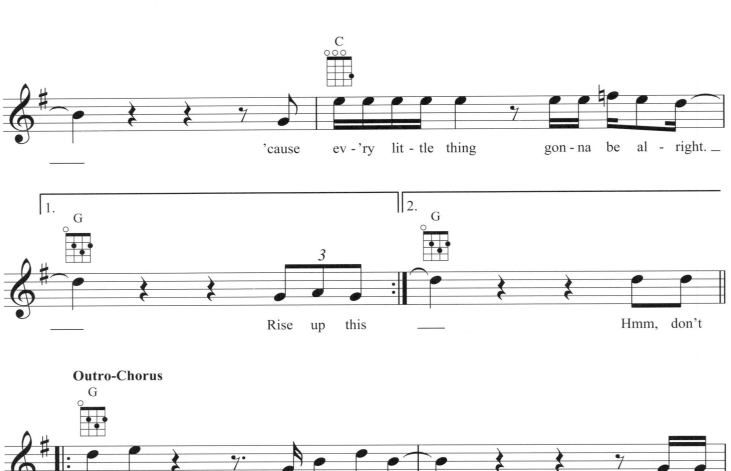

'cause ev-'ry lit-tle thing gon-na be al-right. ___

___

1. Rise up this ___

2. Hmm, don't

Outro-Chorus

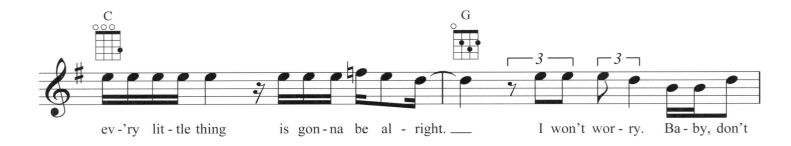

wor-ry a-bout a thing, ___ 'cause, uh,

ev-'ry lit-tle thing is gon-na be al-right. ___ I won't wor-ry. Ba-by, don't

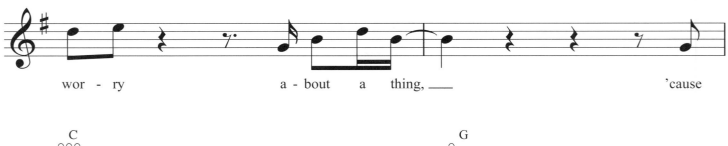

wor-ry a-bout a thing, ___ 'cause

Repeat and fade

ev-'ry lit-tle thing is gon-na be al-right. ___ Say, ___ don't